EDUCATOR'S REFERENCE
FOR
DATA CENTER EDUCATION

A COMPANION TO
"JUMPSTART YOUR CAREER
IN DATA CENTERS"

CARRIE GOETZ

ISBN: 979-8-9873756-2-4 (EBook Educator's Reference)
ISBN: 979-8-9873756-3-1 (Paperback Color Educator's Reference)

Other books in the series
ISBN: 978-1-64184-847-3 (Hardback)
ISBN: 978-1-64184-848-0 (Paperback)
ISBN: 978-1-64184-849-7 (Ebook)
ISBN: 979-8-9873756-0-0 (Hardcover color edition)
ISBN: 979-8-9873756-1-7 (Paperback color edition)

CONTENTS

FORWARD

None of this would be possible without my rock, John. He is my human, and I am eternally grateful.

ABOUT THIS GUIDE

There are multiple exercises in this guide that can be adapted to various classroom grades, homeschooling, scouting technical merit badges, trade and vocational schools, higher education, and employee onboarding exercises. Of course, educators/trainers are free to mix and match. There are a variety of resources to help educators with industry topics. This guide is but one. https://www.carriegoetz.com maintains a list of helpful resources for students of all ages. We encourage you to check back often for updates.

If you need someone to speak to your students, we will facilitate those discussions. Please reach out. Additional content is being added to Youtube® continuously, so check there often.

This educators' guide follows the book Jumpstart Your Career in Data Centers Featuring Careers for Women, Trades, and Veterans in Tech and Data. Centers. You may request a color copy of the illustrations in PDF format at the website listed above. In addition, the book is available electronically, in audio format with author notes, and print (black and white and color). If you can't afford the reader to go along, feel free to at least request a free copy of the illustrations, but the book is HIGHLY recommended.

If you are using this guide for self-instruction, good for you! I hope this is the start of a fantastic career for you. Many of the exercises can be self-completed. Don't skip ones you feel may not be of interest, as there is an overall understanding that is helpful. Give them a try!

BACKGROUND AND TERMS

This section discusses what a data center is and the different silos of operation. Important takeaways are:

- Data centers are where EVERY known digitally documented thing, piece of correspondence, internet communications, and application data lives. Students should understand that just because something is no longer on their device, it still lives in a data center.
- Mission Critical is the industry that builds, supports, operates, and upgrades data centers. However, the industry is so much more than just IT things. Construction, real estate, marketing, accounting, sales, etc., are all part of making the industry work.
- Jobs in the industry encompass so much more than writing code. Jobs include everything from construction to the cloud. Have a visit from a design/build firm to discuss all the types of people they hire. Help students understand that some jobs require a degree and some do not. Some jobs offer a better work/life balance; some are great for people that thrive on chaos. Some have much lower time demands.

BUILDING A HUMAN DATA CENTER

Young students can dress up as the various "roles" listed. Older students simply stand in a circle understanding their role. You will need a tennis ball or something to symbolize the packets being passed. Dividing a larger conversation into smaller "packets" is helpful for more advanced groups. Each packet carrying a piece of the message should be sequentially numbered as it sends and reassembled in order at the opposite end. For every packet that travels in one direction, an acknowledgment travels back to the user. This example helps learners visualize how the Internet works and where data centers fit in conversations. As students are comfortable with the flow of things, you may wish to use multiple tennis balls at once, symbolizing multiple conversations moving at once.

Materials Needed: Tennis balls to symbolize packets, signs for the various roles or costumes to help with visualization, an area for learners to stand (or multiple areas for multiple "data centers,") optional string to show how the individual components are tied together. You can tailor this exercise to your needs. You may use pictures of the actual equipment as well.

- Data center operations are the teams that run data centers. This exercise provides a great visual of how traffic moves and how these departments work together. Use a tennis ball or object to represent the packet as it moves through the facility.

- Sender – pick a few students to be endpoints (laptops or phones). Some will be inside the company's "data center," and some will be outside. These students will initiate the conversations and receive acknowledgments.
- Network delivery people/mail carriers – pick a few students to be delivery persons. They will decide what route the "packet" takes to get to the router. Some network (people) components will be inside the data center, and some will be on another network outside the data center. You can make this exercise as intricate and complex as students can grasp. Multiple networks help understand more complex scenarios.
- Routers are like traffic cops or doormen. They decide which packets stay inside the data center and which leave to the outside world. They also determine what can come into the data center. The router is flanked by firewalls that inspect the packets on both sides of the router.
- Firewalls – the bodyguards/inspectors that protect the traffic cops /doorkeepers above look at the packets and decide if they are safe to stay or leave. This concept may be difficult for early elementary. Just know that there are devices designed to keep them as safe as possible. But note there are always people trying to find their way around them.
- Internet – is the highway department, so to speak. The Internet is comprised of communication lines, routers, and networks, but we will use it as a single entity for now. More advanced classes may wish to break students into various internet segments and decide the best ways to route information.
- Server (waitstaff/servers) – the computer that takes and gives instructions inside the data center. Think of waitstaff at a restaurant.

- Storage – Librarian/file cabinets. The location where things are written down and kept. In a data center, this is hard drives either inside a server or as a standalone subsystem. These devices store information in at least one place until the information is purposefully deleted. Note that not all copies are simultaneously deleted unless you set them to. Data at once facility can remain for years after other copies are deleted.

- For this exercise, you should have both internal and external networks. It may be helpful to group students into circles representing inside the data center and outside of the data center. You can easily do this by putting students in different circles representing disparate networks. Circles work best as students can see and work with each other to start mapping out conversation flows. These are simplistic scenarios but do a great job of helping people understand the complexity of conversations. You can add string, floor tape, signs, etc., to aid learning. You may wish to consolidate some of the tasks above for early elementary students. To help with learning, you may want them to dress up for enhanced visual learning.

While this exercise may seem better suited to younger students, it is also a great way to teach grownups. Let the students sort out the flow with some guidance in the activity. You will find they learn from each other and communicate with each other to sort out the flow.

TECHNICAL DIARIES

Have students keep technical diaries throughout this exercise. For example, students should keep track of their time online, the number of transmissions, streaming minutes, etc. These will be used for various activities throughout the book. In addition, the diary will help students learn about their energy consumption and become aware of their data carbon footprint.

For students who are too young or don't have devices, you can model using averages listed online or charts like the following from localiq.com. There are many examples of what happens in an internet minute.

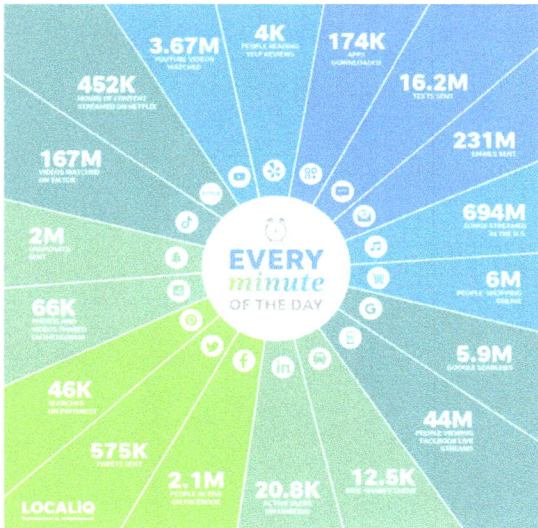

WHAT HAPPENS IN AN INTERNET MINUTE? COURTESY OF LOCALIQ

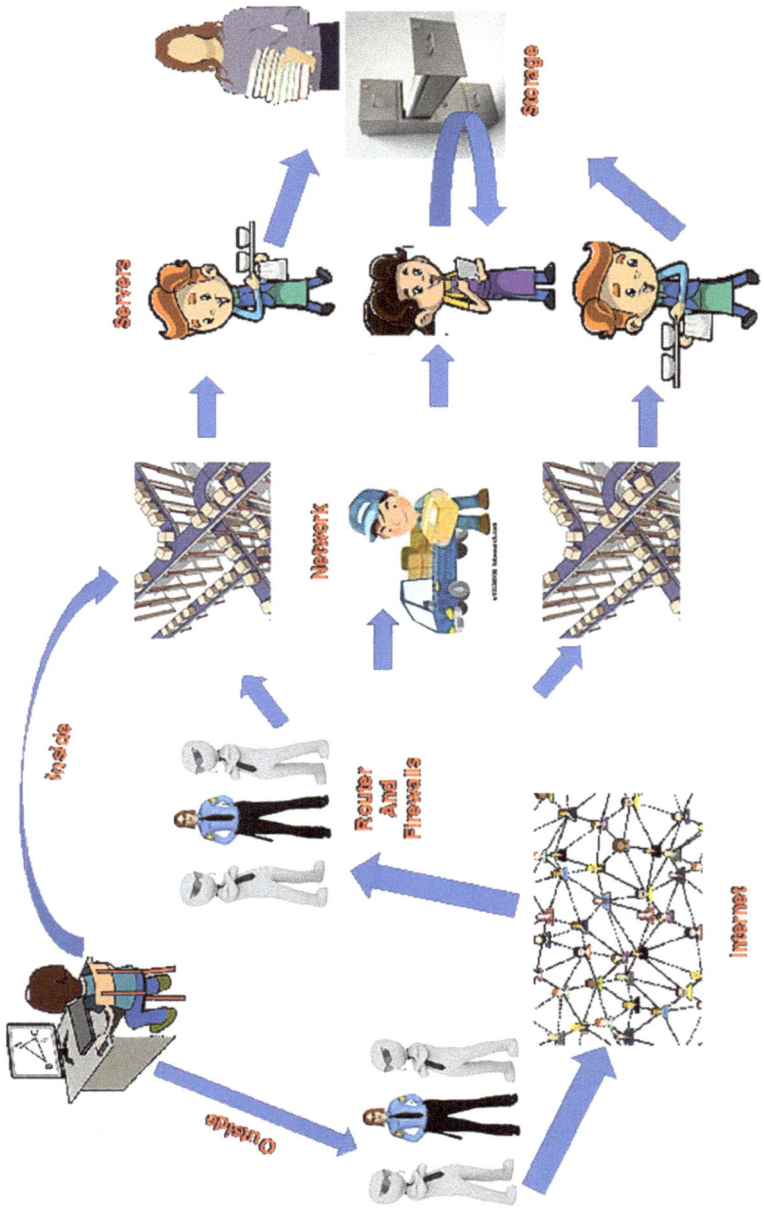

BUILDING A HUMAN DATA CENTER

- A typical internal "conversation" would look like this:
  1. The sender is going to send an email inside the company.
  2. The sender hands off the "packets" of the email to the network.
  3. The network decides how to get the packets to the server.
  4. The server takes the packets and passes the message to storage for safekeeping.
  5. The storage takes the "packet" and holds it until someone else requests it.
  6. The network sends back an acknowledgment packet so the sender knows the packet arrived.
  7. Next, another requester sends "receive my email" to the server via their "packet."
  8. Their packet goes to the network to get to the server.
  9. The server requests the email from storage (the other packet).
  10. Storage hands it to the server.
  11. The server sends it over the network.
  12. Finally, the network hands it back to requester #2.
- An email to an outside person would look like this:
  1. The sender will send an email to someone outside of the company.
  2. The sender hands off the "packet" to the internal network.
  3. The inside network decides how to get the packet to the server.
  4. The server takes the packet and passes the message to storage for safekeeping.
  5. The storage takes the email and holds it until someone else requests it.
  6. An outside requester sends "receive my email" to the server via their "packet."
  7. Their packet goes to their separate inside network.
  8. Their network sees this request is for a destination (address) outside of the local network. So, the packet goes to the firewalls and router.

9. The firewalls inspect to be sure it is free from malware and viruses and then hands the packet off to the router. The router sees that it is outside the data center and OK to transmit, so it hands it off to the firewall facing the Internet.
10. The outside firewall hands it to the internet.
11. The Internet uses its routers and network to get the packet to the data center holding the message (original network).
12. That router and its firewall (bodyguards) check the packet and hand it to the network inside the data center.
13. The inside network hands it to the server.
14. The server hands the request for the email to storage (librarian).
15. Librarian/Storage finds the email and hands the email back to the server.
16. The server sends it over the internal network to the data center router.
17. The data center router/firewalls check the email and sends it to the Internet.
18. The Internet hands it back to the original outside router.
19. That router and bodyguards check the packet and hand it to the local network.
20. The network hands it back to requester #2.
21. Requester #2 opens the email.

- Have students work out what happens when requester #2 replies to the email.
- Have students work out what happens if someone saves from an application.
- How many conversations can students support at once? Where is the bottleneck?

You can build upon these exercises and make them as intricate as necessary. Repetition is key. You can change out students in the various roles. You can add additional circles both inside and outside of the data center. What if one data center talks to another? How does the traffic flow? Think of various conversations and have students sort out how they would flow. What if a student simply saves a photo to the cloud? How do large conversations flow? What about Voice calls over the Internet (just like data packets, but they carry digitized voice)?

UNDERSTANDING WHO DOES WHAT IN A DATA CENTER

Now that students understand the flow of information look at the section at the back of the book and have students discuss which jobs fit into the various stages of a data center build. Suggested activities:

- Have students research various job descriptions and list the differences and likenesses between employers. What are the core responsibilities?
- Have students research employers that are hiring for various positions. What does the company do? Where do they fit in the data center cycles: Design, Site Selection, Build, Operations, Remediation, more than one, etc?

TYPES OF DATA CENTERS

Discuss the various types of data centers and when each could be used. There aren't a lot of right and wrong answers, as companies can take advantage of several models at once, but there are times when companies will only select specific types of data centers. Discuss some of the following examples:

- Pharmaceutical companies – some will be in data centers that are not accessible to the Internet to protect trade secrets. However, some portions of their data will be accessible, like their sales systems, etc. Discuss some other systems they may have and where the control of those systems may be, as in cloud, edge, colo, company-owned, and why.
- Government systems – some will be secret, some not secret, and some must comply with data sovereignty requirements. Help students learn what data sovereignty means and what is considered personally identifiable information the government has on us (tax returns, for instance).
- Manufacturing – Help students understand the types of information gathered in manufacturing. What data is stored versus what is used for machines to communicate that won't need long-term storage? How do factories record information from the machines that run in the factories? Would they need to retain that information long-term or short-term? What information could be saved and help the manufacturing process?

- Retail – Customer purchases need to be tracked for credit cards and inventory. What are the different requirements for each type of transaction? For example, does the company need to know individual sales or just totals from the store? What information is required for inventory versus credit card billing? Where should the information reside?
- Hospitals and medical records – What is unique to these types of digital records? How are they stored, and what protections are needed to ensure that sensitive medical information is not accidentally shared? Do all doctors need to see all patients' records? How are patients charged, and what information is required to add to the charges on a medical record?

For younger students, the important thing to grasp is the privacy needs of information and what information is dangerous if it gets out. Help students learn what is personally identifiable information. What information about them is unique from everyone else?

UNDERSTANDING THE DATA CENTER ORGANIZATION

While every data center is unique in some ways, most organizations will have (or use) the listed departments and personnel to run and maintain a data center. Each specialty has unique responsibilities within the data center ecosystem. If a company wishes to house its data center somewhere other than its office, it will want to know which data centers have these specialties in-house versus outsourced. For enterprises running their own data centers, these departments and jobs will be in-house and generally located near the facility. For each one of the specialties, students can look up job descriptions to find out what each position is responsible for in their daily activities. How do the job descriptions differ for the different types of data center companies? How do the job descriptions change based on the employer? What characteristics and requirements are the same across different providers?

- Set up a data center organization.
- Have students communicate what they do in the various roles.
- Follow a communication thread and have students say what their part is supporting the conversation.
  - *I work on the server team, and we ensure the information is handed out to a requester. Next, we evaluate whether the requester has the right to view the data. Next, we size and test servers to be sure they will support our applications. Finally, we set up the cybersecurity for each server.*

- *I work on the networking team. We make sure that the communications flow through the network. We make sure that each device has a. unique address so that it can communicate.*
- *Telecoms make sure that the communications channels are functional and sized correctly. In addition, telecoms/voice teams ensure that the phone and fax lines work for a company. Sometimes this department also is. Responsible for the cabling plant and phones.*
- *Storage teams organize and maintain the data that is stored within the organization. They determine how long information is held and are responsible for making sure that permissions are up to date and the data is secure. In addition, they help size and determine the amount of storage for each user or application and the type of storage used.*
- *CIO/CTO – the bosses that control the data center or company's data. Discuss how this role is different if a company owns a data center versus leasing it. In addition, the CIO/CTO helps determine where the data centers will be. What are some factors they may use to help determine what their data center footprint will look like? How do the CIO/CTO roles differ?*
- *Cybersecurity teams are responsible for the overall security of networks, data, and systems and work with physical security teams. What are some examples of cybersecurity? What could happen when they go wrong? Talk about recent security breaches and how they could have been stopped/caught.*
- *What positions require or don't require a degree? First, look online and see what employers require for various jobs. Then, have students work through different job descriptions from multiple companies and develop **one combined** that would apply to all of them. The idea is to help students see that job descriptions vary from company to company. But many of the skills needed*

are the same. Which skills do students think would keep them from getting the job? What skills do they think they could learn on the job?

CODES AND STANDARDS

Have students know and be able to identify the difference between a code and a standard. What standards are they likely to use? Have students look up the Ethernet Alliance and some other standard bodies mentioned.

- Write a report on one standard and tell why it is essential.
- What do code officials do?
- What is a certificate of occupancy, and why do you need one?
- What are fire codes, and why are they necessary?
- What happens when there is a code violation?
- What happens if there is a standard violation?
- Interview a code inspector with the class. How did they get their training? What part of their job is most important? How does it protect public safety?

SITE SELECTION

This chapter helps discover what goes into selecting a data center site. There are requirements for a site to have (or be able to get) enough power, fiber/telecommunications, and land for a data center project. How is this different from a company putting its data center in its office building? How would the selection vary from selecting a colocation space? How would the areas be the same? Some examples are:

- *The building must accommodate the same facility resources as a standalone facility.*
- *The building would still need power capacity and fiber, regardless. However, power and cooling needs will price out differently in an office building than in a colocation facility. How would you separate the power bill? Adding a separate meter for the data center will help with efficiency projects.*
- *Cooling systems may differ for a whole office building versus a purpose-built data center.*
- *All systems are under the company's control, versus power, cooling, and floorspace being controlled by a colocation owner.*
- *Separate metering may or may not be available. However, separate metering is encouraged to help gauge power usage.*
- *The company only rents/owns a single space if the data center is in their building. The company rents multiple areas (office and data center) if its data center is not located within its office.*

- *The company won't have to buy generators, chillers, and large capital equipment in a colocation facility.*
- *The company may not be allowed to operate at a lower level of redundancy than is offered at a colocation facility.*
- Have students look at a map of your state or country. What areas seem to be suitable for a data center?
  - *Look at cities that have lots of resources. Why do you think most data center cities are also NFL cities? What advantages do they have over smaller cities (i.e., people, infrastructure, power resources, etc.)? What risk factors exist within or near the area?*
- Help them find fiber maps for fiber paths. How else can telecommunications work other than fiber? How fast can they operate?
  - *Cellular, regular phone lines, 5G, Wireless, Line of Site, etc., all will have different speeds and capabilities. Have students put together a comparison chart of the various carriers and capabilities. Why is one better than the other? Why would you use one to back up the other? What is the cost per mile to install fiber infrastructure in your area?*
- Look at the primary data center cities identified in the book. What power makeup do they have compared to the power sources for your city?
  - *Have students research power sources for some cities in your state. How much power does your state use? What is the carbon footprint of that power? Using the power makeup in your state/area, what is the power usage for technology of any student on any day? You will use the diaries created earlier.*
- How much land would be required for 100MW of solar? 100MW of wind? How far would the footprint stretch on the map?
  - *Using the calculations from the class, how much power total do they use just for computing? How much land would be required to generate that power via solar and wind?*

- What local hindrances to solar and wind occur?
  - *What are the downsides of solar and wind? Would they work year-round? What climate issues need consideration?*
  - *How many days of the year are sunny/windy? How do you supply power when the sun isn't shining, and the wind isn't blowing?*
- Have students determine the best area for renewables in your state.
- Have students determine the power cost for each city based on various loads. Help students understand demand fees and transmission fees.
  - *Students should be able to convert a kW into a kW/hour.*
  - *Have students understand their power bill as part of this exercise.*
  - *Explain demand charges and transmission fees seen on commercial bills.*
  - *What are peak charges, and how would you avoid them? How could you decrease them? What could make each fee increase?*
  - *Invite a representative from the power company to discuss commercial power and renewables.*
- When would you want services in a particular city instead of another? Latency? What other location concerns come to mind?
  - *Have students understand latency by handing off a packet. Time the transmission as it is handed off from student to student with 5 participants. Repeat with 20. Each student represents a hop on the Internet (handoff from one device to another). How can you increase the speed from point A to point B? Increase the telecommunications speed, decrease the number of hops, etc. Where are the hops on the Internet? Run a Tracert in a command window on a laptop (traceroute in a terminal window on a Mac) to any website. Try a few to see the differences. Some firewalls will stop the outgoing packet, but you will still see the hop. Each represents a router on the Internet. You will see each hop of the conversation as the Internet traces the packet. Have students try to identify the hops.*

- What is a microgrid? How does it differ from a substation? What are the kinds of microgrids available?
  - *Microgrids can supply energy to consumers on the grid and in island mode (standalone). It can provide power TO the grid as well. Nuclear, natural gas, carbon sequestered natural gas, carbon captured natural gas, solar, wind, hydroelectric, etc., are all options. Have students create science projects on various types of power sources. Which are renewable?*

METHODOLOGIES FOR UPTIME

Uptime refers to the availability of resources on the Internet. Uptime includes the IT gear (servers, networking, storage, etc.) and the facilities (power, cooling, infrastructure) portions. Redundancy is the methodology used for facilities, and resiliency is used for computing components. Both are comprised of various duplicate components for failover.

- Use a simple battery backup to explain redundancy. For example, what happens when you unplug power? How long does the battery last? When do you actually go down?
- Have students look up the various types of batteries. How are their components sourced? What countries do they come from? Do they have a circular economy life? (Can they be used for residential or other purposes when they no longer meet the needs of a data center?)
- What happens when the battery runs out? How does a generator kick in? How does it know?
  - *Have students look up switch gear and report on the function.*
  - *Have students look up three companies that make power components for a data center. What does each of them do?*
- Have students discuss the importance of resiliency versus redundancy. For example, if the power is always up, will you ever need redundant components on the computing side? Why or why not?

- *Have students work up some typical applications from their diaries. What happens to each if they can't access the application for a given period? What is the recourse? What applications need a higher level of resiliency and redundancy? Resiliency can be exampled by accessing the application on another phone, the same data via another resource. Do you know where your servers are when you access them via an application?*

- Scope 1, 2, and 3 emissions refer to a company's carbon footprint. Have students determine their emissions based on home usage. What is the power source makeup in their community? Do they utilize solar in their home? What would be the advantage of doing so? How much could their home save? Could they use servers in another town to lower their emissions? Where would be the best location to do so?

  - *Have students look at the Department of Energy (https://www.doe.gov) website and see what they can learn about your state/community.*
  - *What are green credits? What do power companies do with them?*
  - *Invite someone in the solar or wind industries to speak to your class.*

- Where does carbon come from, and when is it beneficial? How do we capture carbon? What can we do with carbon once it is captured?

  - *Sequestration or capture and reuse are both viable options for carbon. Have students discover beneficial uses of carbon. For example, how do planting trees take help the environment? How would students offset their carbon usage?*

COOLING AND
WATER BASICS

Cooling is a critical part of the data center ecosystem. While technically, we are removing heat; the byproduct is still a cooler environment. There are two ways to cool. One is with air movement; the other involves liquid absorbing heat. At this point, students need to get an understanding of water conservation. Each area of the country is different, but help students understand drought versus rainforest. What happens when water is scarce? If water is a critical element in cooling, what happens when there isn't water? What environmental events impact water supply?

PHYSICAL SECURITY

There are many jobs in security in the data center industry. In general, they are divided into physical security and cybersecurity. For physical security, it is fun to have students explore various locations they know and determine what could make the land and area more secure. Fencing, security guards, etc., are all a part of securing and maintaining security at any site. Invite some police or security guards to your class to talk about the importance of crime prevention. Invite someone working for a security camera or biometrics company to do a class demonstration.

DCS FOR BEES

While this is a bit off-topic, conservation is a big part of our industry. Help students understand the importance of pollinators and how we can help our food supply by adding pollinator space to our data center campuses. See if a local data center will allow students to plant flowers for pollinators. What pollinators are local to your region? Grow some pollinator plants at school.

OVERALL ECOSYSTEM

The idea here is to help students understand the entire data center environment is an ecosystem. In this case, an ecosystem is defined as a complex network of interconnected systems. The failure of one component can cause others to fail.

- What makes up an ecosystem? How is it different from a data center? How is it alike?
    - *What is the definition of an ecosystem? How are the parts dependent upon the other parts?*
- Name some other ecosystems like grassland, tundra, and desert. What parts are interdependent upon other parts?
- How does improving one part of an ecosystem improve other parts?
- The three main ecosystems in the data center are power, cooling, and compute. So, what happens if any of them fail?
- Understand PUE (Power Usage Effectiveness). What does the equation mean?
    - *The equation is used to understand how much power is used to support facilities versus IT load. It is overall building power/IT load. The closer to 1, the better. A data center with a 1 PUE would mean that all the power supplied is operating without loss or waste and wholly in support of the center's computing. It is not feasible, but indeed a goal. The idea is to get the systems supporting the IT load with as little waste as possible.*

- What steps can be taken to ensure power usage is as efficient as possible?
  - *Turn off lights, ensure air units are working at their optimal efficiency, and use the most efficient power supplies.*
  - *Have students look up Energy Star ratings for power supplies. What do they notice for differences between the various kinds?*
  - *How can students lower their power bills at home?*
- TheGreenGrid.org has some great whitepapers on this topic. Have students look up some of their supplied information and report on the problem being addressed.
- Understand greenfield (brand new) versus brownfield (partially or fully constructed and about to be remediated). What are the different considerations for each environment?
- What existing conditions could impact decisions? Some examples are:
  - *Building height and ceiling height will impact the height of cabinets and the ability to add a raised floor if desired. Although elevators may limit equipment and cabinet decisions, seismic loading may also affect these decisions.*
  - *Physical floor space restrictions may limit the number of cabinets or cages placed on the floor.*
  - *Roof and floor loading may need attention.*
  - *Existing power to the building may or may not need to be increased.*
- Power equates to cooling needs.
  - *Watts x 3.41 BTU/hour*
- How does a higher power draw increase cooling needs?
- Have students look up the ASHRAE tables for data center temperatures and humidity.
- What happens when the temperature of the data hall is increased or decreased?

- Have students learn about the Tier rating systems as an explanation of redundant components. For example, what happens when power is one Tier and cooling is another? What good do the tiers do?
  - *The tier levels, grades, and others are a means to identify which components are backed up (redundant) and to what level using standard terminology. Note: "Designed to" and "built to" may not be the same.*
  - *Facilities are rated to their lowest-performing components. For instance, Tier 3 cooling and Tier 4 power will give the facility an overall Tier 3 rating.*
- Look up voltages around the globe. Help students understand the different types of power and power outlets internationally. Who is responsible for making sure power is safe and properly connected?
  - *The AHJ – Authority Having Jurisdiction*
  - *Identify your AHJs in your area. Then, have one come and talk to the class.*
  - *Help the class understand what an AHJ contributes to safety.*
- What happens if you double the number of computers in a space? What happens if you cut the number in half?
  - *The power and cooling will change with the compute load.*
  - *You cannot add more computing than you have power or cooling to support.*
  - *You can have enough power but not enough cooling. In this case, the cooling is the limiting factor. Therefore, you must either add cooling capacity or not install the additional computing without retiring some other power load.*
  - *Without enough power or cooling, additional computing would need to be installed elsewhere, spun up in the cloud, or some means to add power/cooling capacity must occur.*

PUTTING IT ALL TOGETHER SO FAR

Several engineering and architectural firms work in the data center space. Some work on the sustainability side, while others focus on other areas. Design and construction are both imperative to a well-functioning facility. Pick a spot for a data center to cover with the class. You may wish to have half the class start on a greenfield project and half on a brownfield. Have students define:

- Civil engineering
- Structural engineering
- MEP (Mechanical, Electrical, Plumbing)
- LEED
- BREEAM
- Net Zero
- Sustainability Coordinator
- Physical Security
- Building Envelope
- What part of the construction process do you think would involve each?
- Where would these individuals get ideas for size and scope? What departments would they involve in discussions?
- What unique considerations do students think would be necessary for special circumstances? Common defense/Department of

Defense? Doctor's office? Tax forms? Movie streaming? Is all the data the same even within any of the above?

- What is a Faraday cage? What is a SCIF?
- What is an edge data center? When would it be used?

Use the diagram below and be able to discuss each section and why it is essential.

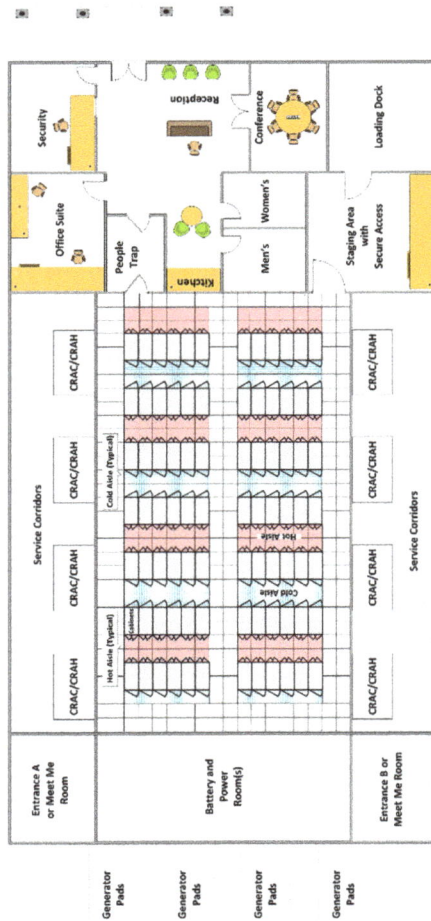

- Help students understand the equipment listed in this chapter.
- Invite service or sales personnel for some equipment to speak to the class. They can provide an overview of the technology and its purpose. Alternatively, a data center provider would be a great guest.
- What happens if some of these areas don't exist? How would that change operations and security?
- Why do students think some of the areas are separate?

INTERNET OF THINGS

The Internet of Things (IoT) refers to all our connected devices. Ask each student to count up all of the devices they have that are connected, including thermostats, lights, Bluetooth music, and anything else with an address that they can talk to via an app. Are there sensors involved? The number can be an eye-opener! What are some creative uses for sensors? How could sensors save a company money?

LIGHTING PROTECTION

Understanding the purpose behind lighting protection can be a fun science experiment, but it is beyond the scope here. Lighting protection may be outside at your ball field or on top of your building. Alternatively, there will be some protection on large towers. How do taller metal objects attract lightning?

PARTICULARS OF POWER DELIVERY

The relationship between power, cooling, and compute are the main components from design through operations. The relationship between the three is the core of the data center ecosystem functionality. Power is essential to uptime. Understanding backup power components will go far in helping students understand how the power flows. You can't trace electrons to the energy source unless you generate the power or specify the source through a power purchasing agreement. But each component will have some place in sustainability. Different equipment will have different power efficiencies.

- Have students look up each component listed in the book and define its purpose.
- Have students understand waste and power efficiency.
- Have students list some critical selection criteria for their assigned component.
- Have students discuss what happens should their assigned component fail.
- How does the data center stay working?
- How do power storage components store power? For how long?
- Helping students understand how generators kick in when the power goes out is essential. Some students may have generators at home.

- *The switchgear is responsible for switching the power from one source to another. Some are automatic, some manual. What are the differences in capabilities? What is arc flash?*
- What could cause the power to fail? Have students list not just storms, etc., but which components failing would cause an outage?
- How would things be different if there was only one power feed?
- How would equipment work without a secondary power supply?
- Create a model with colored string or yarn to show the various power components connected. Use different colors for each power feed. One color for primary and one for secondary help visualize the transmission paths.
- Help students understand how additional levels of redundancy in components can provide additional uptime.

DESIGN AND CONSTRUCTION

In this exercise, students can create their own data center building. The "building" can be made from legos, cardboard, or any other suitable material. You can use the diagram above and in the book to help students plan for each space. For the site, have students create a plan on a map for where it all will start. What does the site layout look like?

- Have groups of students start a data center model.
- Have them pick a site and explain why they chose it. Things to consider include the following:
  - *Overall data center size*
  - *Room for generators, chillers, underground tanks, etc.*
  - *Climate to help determine the best type of cooling/heat rejection equipment.*
  - *Distance to fiber carriers or central offices.*
  - *Available power and distance to substations or the available land to build power infrastructure.*
- Have them list the needed services and investigate potential companies to supply the labor and materials. What is required to manage multiple companies? What will the major steps in construction be? Invite construction personnel to discuss their roles with the class.
- What materials are they going to need to get started?
- What is the power makeup for the site? Will renewables be an option? What about carbon capture?

- Have students list some jobs involved in engineering, construction, drafting, etc., that will be needed. Younger students may want to dress as these professions and provide a report for what each does. What skills are required? What is the typical workday?
- Have a construction workday at school and invite people within those industries to speak to the class.
- If possible, visit a construction site or show a video of the construction process.
- Have students outline their physical security strategy for the site.
- How will outside temperatures impact the building envelope?
- How will the environment for the site dictate construction?
  - *Snow?*
  - *Earthquakes?*
  - *Tornadoes?*
  - *Airports?*
  - *Highways?*
  - *City services?*
- What kind of data center are they building? How many users? Is there a particular purpose?
  - *Edge*
  - *Colo*
  - *Cloud/Wholesale*
  - *Enterprise*
- How is their power sourced? What would they expect in a power purchasing agreement? What sources would they use for energy?

Pick an assumed amount of power or have the students estimate expected power needs. Most data centers are built knowing the power or with an estimate of overall power in expectation of tenants or current needs plus growth.

- What is the difference between DC and AC power? Which equipment uses each? Which equipment switches between the two?
- How much room is needed for each piece of heavy equipment (generators, etc.) on the site?
- Have students look up Tier levels and discuss what each means for redundancy. Which components need to be redundant for each? Is the cost justified? What would make a data center use any particular level of redundancy? How do the Tier levels vary from Category and downtime expectations? What other sectors can you think of that could benefit from redundancy?
- How many carriers will they need in their meet-me-rooms? Note: Communications also need to be resilient. What are the requirements for entrance facilities? What is a meet-me-room?
- Have students look up mantraps, biometrics, and other security mechanisms and report on them.
- Have an engineering firm come and talk to the students about some of the considerations.
- How many systems can students name that will be a part of the building monitoring?
- Have students read their meters at their homes. How much power does their home use in a day? Based on their power source, what is their carbon footprint?
- For younger students, have them "earn" power for communications. For instance, have students walk around a desk ten times to send a message to the class data center. Have students "earn" power to transmit messages by decreasing power for other things. For instance, if students want to send an email, have them lose 3 minutes of TV time to make up for the power usage.

DCIM

Data center infrastructure management helps data centers monitor power usage and spare capacity and ensure adequate cooling across the floor. Capabilities of these systems vary from supplier to supplier. Some systems are closed (they only work with specific equipment). While other systems are "open," meaning they work with a variety of equipment without proprietary or equipment-specific requirements.

- Schedule a demo for the class from a DCIM vendor.
- Visit a data center and look at their DCIM systems in their NOC.
- Have students compare 3 different DCIM products. What are the similarities and differences?
- Why would a facility need this level of monitoring?
  - *Set up a class row of "cabinets" boxes. For each box, place ten blue marbles and ten red marbles to represent power connections for primary and secondary. Have students act as equipment. If a student only needs primary power, they get one blue marble. Students who need both primary and secondary will receive one of each marble. This represents power design and commissioning (simplified).*
  - *What happens when the marbles are gone? How would you connect another piece of equipment? Explain decommissioning by retiring equipment and reassigning the marbles. What happens if the marbles get out of control? Suppose one student gets two blue marbles. How would they work if red marbles were in power?*

- *What if some students need more marbles (power)? What does that do to the number of students supported?*
- *Have students hold up their primary (blue) marbles. What are red marbles doing? What could you use them for while still guaranteeing that they can provide power if the blue goes down? What do you call the marbles on standby? This is stranded power. Power that is allocated but not used.*
- *What happens when a "computer" needs only half a marble? The student still gets the full marble, but some marble capacity is wasted (also stranded).*
- *Add blue and red marbles to signify additional capacity. How do you know how many to give to each student? Some students will need more than one marble for bigger (more power hungry) equipment. Not all equipment draws the same amount of power.*

COOLING TECHNOLOGIES

The easiest way to demonstrate how cooling works is through some fun experimentation.

You will need some strip thermometers, a hair dryer or lamp (heat source), a clear box, or a box with plastic wrap on one side. As with any experiment, be sure to have adult supervision. Pairing with a science class for some of these may be fun. Help students understand the different cooling/heat rejection types and explain the pros and cons of the various systems. For example, why is water better than air? When would it not be a good idea to use water?

Explain Water Usage Effectiveness.

> *Water Usage Effectiveness (WUE) is a metric used to evaluate the efficiency of water usage in data centers. It measures the amount of water consumed by a data center in relation to the amount of water used specifically for cooling purposes. WUE provides insights into the data center's water management and helps identify opportunities for improving water efficiency.*

The formula for calculating Water Usage Effectiveness (WUE) is as follows:

> *WUE = Total annual site water consumption (liters) / IT equipment annual energy consumption (kWh)*

In this formula:

Total annual site water consumption refers to the amount of water used by the data center for all purposes, including cooling, maintenance, and other operational needs, measured in liters.

IT equipment annual energy consumption represents the total energy consumed by the IT equipment within the data center over the course of a year, measured in kilowatt-hours (kWh).

A lower WUE value indicates more efficient water use in cooling the data center's IT equipment. It suggests that the data center is using less water to dissipate heat from the IT equipment, resulting in improved water efficiency. It is important to note that there is a tradeoff when water is not used for heat rejection. Electrical usage will be higher.

To improve the WUE value, data centers can implement various water conservation measures, such as:

- *Implementing more efficient cooling systems that reduce the reliance on water for cooling, such as using air-side economizers or other liquid cooling technologies.*
- *Optimizing cooling system operations and controls to ensure cooling resources are used only when necessary and in the most efficient manner.*
- *Reusing or recycling water within the data center, such as using treated wastewater or captured rainwater for cooling purposes. Not all jurisdictions allow trapping rainwater.*
- *Implementing leak detection and repair programs to minimize water wastage.*
- *Monitoring and analyzing water usage patterns to identify areas for improvement and implement targeted water-saving strategies.*

- *By measuring and improving the Water Usage Effectiveness (WUE), data centers can enhance their sustainability efforts and reduce the environmental impact associated with water consumption.*

Experiment: Basic principles of air conditioning:

Materials needed:

Two identical cups, ice cubes, water, a thermometer, plastic wrap or a balloon, a rubber band, or string

Procedure:

- Fill one cup with room-temperature water.
- Place a few ice cubes in the other cup.
- Measure and record the initial temperature of both cups using a thermometer.
- Cover the cup with ice cubes using plastic wrap or a balloon, securing it with a rubber band or string to create an airtight seal.
- Wait for about 10-15 minutes.
- After the waiting period, measure and record the temperature of both cups again.

Explanation:

- The cup with ice cubes represents the evaporator coil in an air conditioning system, while the cup with water represents the ambient air in a room. The process involves the evaporation and condensation of water, similar to how air conditioning works.

When you cover the cup with ice, the ice absorbs heat from the surrounding air, causing the water in the cup to evaporate. Evaporation is a cooling process that requires energy (in this case, heat) to change water from a liquid to a gas. The heat energy from the surrounding air is used to convert the water into water vapor.

As the water evaporates, heat energy is removed from the cup and surrounding air, causing the temperature to drop. This cooling effect is similar to what happens in the evaporator coil of an air conditioning system. The evaporator coil contains a refrigerant that evaporates, absorbing heat from the indoor air.

When you compare the temperatures of the two cups, you should observe that the cup with the ice cubes has a lower temperature compared to the cup with room temperature water. This experiment demonstrates the cooling effect achieved by the evaporation process, a fundamental principle behind this type of heat rejection/air conditioning.

Heat Rise

Demonstrating the heat rise in a data center can be challenging due to the specialized environment and equipment involved. However, here's a simplified experiment that can help illustrate the concept of heat rising:

Materials needed:

Two different height tall boxes with lids, two hair dryers (same wattage), clear container of liquid, thermometers, or thermometer strips. You may wish to use plastic wrap for the front of the box so that thermometers are easier to read. Measure the temperatures at the red lines. As the experiment looks at heat rise at various locations, the locations do not need to be exact, just roughly halfway and at the top. The glass of water should also change temperature. What is the difference in air temperature rise times without the glass and with the glass?

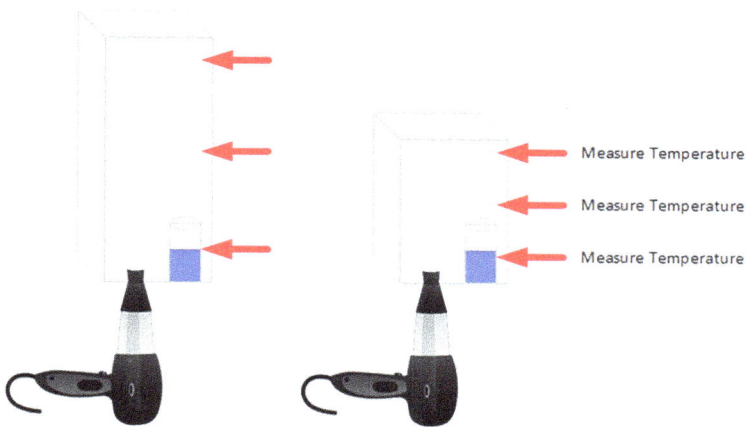

Measure Temperature

Measure Temperature

Measure Temperature

Procedure:

- Cut a hole in the bottom of each box for the hair dryers.
- Place thermometers in each container, ensuring that the thermometer bulb is suspended or the thermometer strips are attached to the sides.
- Try this experiment without the glass of water first. Turn on the hair dryers and monitor the temperatures of all of the thermometers. How much longer does it take for the temperature to rise in each box?
- Add the glasses of water to each box (don't let out the hot air). Allow the water to sit inside each box for 10 minutes. What is the temperature difference in each glass of water? Is there a difference from one box to the next?
- Observe the temperature of each container near the top, and note any temperature differences between the top and bottom.
- Turn the hair dryers back on. Observe the temperatures. What are the differences?
- What happens if you add a cup of ice to each box?

Explanation:

- In a data center, heat is generated by the servers, networking equipment, and other electronics. As these devices operate, they produce heat, which rises due to convection. This experiment aims to demonstrate the basic principle of heat rising. The glasses of water add the ability to observe water attracting heat.

Using the thermometers, you can observe the different temperatures between the containers. The temperature difference demonstrates how hot air tends to accumulate at higher levels.

Remember that this experiment provides a simplified representation and may not fully capture a data center's complex heat dynamics and airflow patterns. Additionally, it's important to emphasize that actual data centers have sophisticated cooling systems designed to manage and dissipate heat effectively.

Air versus Water Experiment 2

To demonstrate the difference between air and water in terms of heat absorption, you can conduct the following experiment:

Materials needed:

Two identical containers (such as glass jars or cups), water, thermometer, and heat source (such as a lamp or sunlight)

Procedure:

- Fill one container with water, leaving some space at the top.
- Leave the other container empty, representing the presence of air.

- Place the containers side by side, equidistant from the heat source (lamp or sunlight).
- Allow both containers equal exposure to the heat source for an equal amount of time.
- Measure and record the temperature of both containers using a thermometer.
- Compare the temperature changes between the container with water and air.

Explanation:

- Water has a higher heat capacity than air, which means it can absorb more heat energy per unit mass. This experiment aims to highlight this difference by observing the temperature changes in the containers.

As the heat source warms up the surroundings, the container with water will absorb the heat energy more effectively compared to the container with air. As a result, the water molecules will gain energy and increase in temperature at a relatively slower rate than the air in the other container.

By comparing the temperature measurements, you should observe that the container with water exhibits a smaller increase in temperature compared to the container with air. This difference demonstrates that water can absorb and retain heat better than air.

Remember to exercise caution when working with heat sources and handle hot objects carefully to prevent burns or accidents.

Containment System Experiment

Hot aisle containment is a technique used in data centers to improve energy efficiency by separating the hot air expelled from servers from the cool air used for cooling. While it may be challenging to replicate the exact conditions of a data center hot aisle containment setup, we can design a simplified experiment to demonstrate the concept using household materials:

Materials needed:

Two cardboard boxes of similar size, plastic wrap or a large plastic sheet, a thermometer, two small fans, a heat source (such as a hairdryer), tape or adhesive

Procedure:

- Set up the two cardboard boxes side by side, leaving a gap between them.
- Create an enclosed space by covering the gap between the boxes and the open ends with plastic wrap or a plastic sheet. Ensure the enclosure is airtight.
- Label one box as the "hot aisle" and the other as the "cold aisle."
- Place a heat source, such as a hairdryer set on high, in the "hot aisle" box.
- Position a small fan at one end of the "hot aisle" box, blowing air towards the heat source. This fan represents the server fans expelling hot air.
- Place the other small fan at one end of the "cold aisle" box, blowing air towards the "hot aisle" box. This fan represents the cooling system.
- Use tape or adhesive to secure the fans in place.

- Wait a few minutes to allow the hot air to accumulate in the "hot aisle" box.
- Measure and record the temperatures in the "hot aisle" and "cold aisle" boxes using a thermometer.
- Compare the temperature differences between the two boxes.
- Explanation:
- In a hot aisle containment setup, the hot air generated by servers is contained in a designated space, separate from the cool air supply. This experiment aims to demonstrate the concept by creating a simplified model.

The hairdryer in the "hot aisle" box represents the heat source generated by servers. The fan blowing air towards the heat source mimics the server fans' airflow that expels hot air into the hot aisle.

The other box, the "cold aisle," represents the area where cool air is supplied to the servers. The fan in this box represents the cooling system, which delivers cool air to the servers. You may use the hair dryer on the cold setting in the cold aisle. What happens when you remove the barrier? How do the temperatures change? What if you change the cycle from hot to cold on the hair dryers? How does the air mix change?

While this experiment provides a basic understanding of the concept of hot aisle containment, it's important to note that the setup in an actual data center is more complex and involves advanced cooling systems and airflow management techniques.

Submersion / Immersion Cooling

This newer cooling method submerses servers in a fluid. The fluid works to remove the heat from the server chips. As water is conductive, it is NOT used for this process. Rather non-dielectric fluid is used. Have students write a report on immersion cooling. What fluids are used?

Rear Door Heat Exchangers

These work similarly to a radiator in a car. Have students understand what a rear door heat exchanger is and its similarity to a radiator. Rear door heat exchangers are a great example of bringing thoughts from one solution to another unrelated area. Innovation never happens in a vacuum.

FIRE SUPPRESSION

Fire detection and suppression are essential parts of any building. Help students understand the various types of fire suppression and how they work.

CFD

There are many examples of computational fluid dynamics. This methodology is used in a variety of industries. Show students images of CFD for clarity.

DESIGN CONSIDERATIONS

Data center design is intricate, and there are multiple solutions, and each will vary based on the power and cooling capacity in the space. It may be helpful to break the students into groups and have them each create a design based on different kW/square foot or kW per cabinet to showcase the differences in design. Students can examine the differences between vertical higher power/higher density cabinets and lower power/lower density cabinets.

Project: Data Center Cabinet and Equipment Layout Design

Objective: The objective of this project is to help students understand the principles of cabinet and equipment layout in a data center, focusing on optimizing space utilization, airflow management, and accessibility.

Steps for the Project:

Research: Instruct students to research best practices and industry standards for cabinet and equipment layout in data centers. They should explore concepts such as rack unit (U) measurements, server and networking equipment dimensions, cabling guidelines, and airflow management techniques.

Requirements Gathering: Define a set of requirements for the data center layout, including the number and type of racks, equipment specifications, power, and cooling requirements, and any specific customer or industry considerations. Students can create a fictional scenario or base it on real-world data center requirements.

> *How will site selection impact their projects? How is the layout of the facility affected by site selection? How much power will be needed for primary and secondary in each cabinet? Will they all be allocated the same amount of power? How do allocations change if there is a high density area?*

Floor Plan and Rack Placement: Provide students with a floor plan or layout of the data center space, including the available rack positions and room dimensions. Alternatively, they can create their own floor plan using software tools or drawing techniques. Next, instruct students to strategically place racks on the floor plan, considering factors such as power distribution, cooling requirements, network connectivity, and accessibility.

> *Did the students select a raised floor or not? Why or why not? If so, what systems will be installed under the floor?*

Equipment Layout: Instruct students to select and position the equipment within the racks, considering their dimensions, power consumption, and heat dissipation characteristics. They should plan for proper airflow management, separating hot and cold aisles, and arranging equipment to minimize heat buildup and optimize cooling efficiency. You may wish to pick some various servers and networking equipment for this exercise, or allow students to select their own.

> *Make sure that students address all types of equipment, including networking, servers, wide area networking, telecommunications, etc. Have students distribute the power to the various cabinets. Have students create a spreadsheet that tracks*

the power requirements for each piece of equipment so that they can allocate resources accordingly. How would they track equipment, addresses, cabling, power, and cooling capacity?

Cable Management: Students should incorporate cable management techniques into their design to ensure neat and organized cabling. They should consider cable routing, cable lengths, labeling, and separation of power and data cables to minimize interference and facilitate easy maintenance and troubleshooting. Students can use varied colored strings (pens) to represent cabling. For instance, you may choose red for primary and green for secondary copper, and yellow and white for primary and secondary fiber. You may choose blue and black for primary and secondary power cables. Select a thicker string for the power.

How would students ensure that the cabling is dressed? How will they document from and to locations? Which cabling will be copper, and which will be fiber? What speeds will they select? Will they use the same speeds everywhere? Explore cabling fails and expert cabling and note the difference. Why would tidiness matter?

Power and Cooling Considerations: Instruct students to plan for power distribution within the cabinets, ensuring proper power load balancing and redundancy. They should consider the positioning of power distribution units (PDUs) and cable routing for efficient power delivery. Students should also include cooling considerations, such as positioning cooling units, implementing airflow management techniques, and planning for adequate ventilation.

What type of cooling is selected and why? Did students choose containment? Why or why not? Did students create a design with the same density everywhere?

Accessibility and Maintenance: Students should ensure that their equipment layout allows easy access and maintenance. They should consider factors such as clearance for equipment removal and replacement, space for technician access, and the use of proper tools and safety measures.

Documentation and Presentation: Students should document their cabinet and equipment layout design, including the floor plan, rack placement diagrams, equipment positioning, cable management plans, and power and cooling considerations. They should present their design to the class, explaining their layout choices and how they addressed the requirements and considerations.

How would they handle labeling and documentation from day one? What would they do for moves, adds, and changes? How would they handle commissioning and decommissioning?

This project enables students to apply their knowledge of cabinet and equipment layout principles in a practical setting. In addition, it allows them to think critically about space optimization, airflow management, and accessibility, which are crucial aspects of data center operations. Collaboration, research, documentation, and presentation skills are also developed throughout the project, mirroring real-world data center design and management scenarios.

UNDERSTANDING ACTIVE EQUIPMENT AND SIZING

Objective: The objective of this project is to help students understand the process of sizing servers and networking equipment for data centers, considering factors such as capacity planning, performance requirements, scalability, and cost optimization.

Steps for the Project:

Research: Instruct students to research the principles and methodologies involved in sizing servers and networking equipment for data centers. They should explore topics such as capacity planning, performance metrics, server specifications, network bandwidth requirements, and industry standards.

Capacity Planning: Define a hypothetical data center scenario or select a real-world case study for the project. Provide students with the necessary information, such as expected workloads, anticipated user demand, and growth projections. Instruct students to determine the required capacity for servers and networking equipment based on the given data.

> *How many concurrent users can use one server? How would things like seasonal fluctuations change the capacity needs?*

Server Sizing: Instruct students to analyze the workload characteristics and performance requirements of the data center. They should select appropriate server configurations, considering factors such as CPU power, memory capacity, storage capacity, and network connectivity. Students should determine the number of servers needed to meet the workload demands, ensuring scalability and considering redundancy and resiliency for fault tolerance.

> *Which is more important? Fault tolerance, redundancy, resiliency, or some combination? Why? What applications need various levels of redundancy? What happens during downtime? How much does downtime cost?*

Networking Equipment Sizing: Students should analyze the network requirements of the data center, including bandwidth needs, latency considerations, and network topology. Instruct them to select networking equipment, such as switches, routers, and firewalls, to handle the anticipated network traffic. They should consider factors like port density, throughput, and features necessary for efficient and secure data transfer. Invite a cabling (copper and/or fiber) manufacturer in to discuss cabling and networking. Invite networking manufacturers to come to class.

> *How fast do networks need to be? Do all segments need to be as fast? Get a map of subsea cables to help students visualize cable paths. How fast is 5G? Now is a great time to examine communications within the data center and in transit into and out of the environment. Maps of satellite communications will also provide some context for extraterrestrial communications. 5G tower maps will likewise provide another visual aid. Students need to know the various means of communications. Have students define bottlenecks, oversubscription, and other networking terms. Explain the OSI stack for students in IT programs. What are protocols? What protocols will you use in your data center? What is the benefit of having different*

networks for different things? What does oversubscription mean and why is it important?

Wide Area Equipment and Firewalls: Students will benefit from gaining an understanding of essential cybersecurity and internet security. This lesson is particularly important. Investigate some cybersecurity events that have been in the headlines. Ask students how many of their parents have identity theft protection plans.

> *Why is cybersecurity so critical? How many ways can students identify threats to their own devices, home networks, etc.? Are passwords enough? What are some cyber threats, and how would they protect against them? What could go wrong? What are some ways that protection can fail? What is zero trust? If students were chief security officers, what steps would they take to ensure their networks remain breach free?*

Scalability and Future Growth: Encourage students to consider future scalability in their equipment sizing. They should analyze growth projections and plan for additional capacity to accommodate increased workloads and user demand. In addition, students should outline strategies for scaling up the server and networking infrastructure.

> *How would students design a network for future growth? Is it less expensive to put it all in at once? What is a good percentage to allow for growth? What limits are too much? What about the category of cabling? How will that impact longevity and speed limits? How does the cost of electronics change with cabling selection change?*

Cost Optimization: Instruct students to balance performance requirements with cost considerations. They should compare different server and networking equipment options, considering factors such as upfront costs, power consumption, maintenance expenses, and total cost of ownership (TCO). Students should aim to optimize the equipment sizing to meet performance needs while staying within budget constraints.

> *Help students figure out computing costs based on a variety of factors such as cost per user-supported, cost per kW/h of power consumption, speed, growth needs, cost to upgrade, etc. For example, what works better from a cost perspective: a centralized network switch or multiple switches?*

Storage: Storage is where data lives. Students should understand the difference between random access memory and permanent/semi-permanent storage. Instruct students to investigate data retention guidelines and data sovereignty laws.

> *What type(s) of storage will students select? How much information will be stored, and for how long? What protocols will storage use? What are the sovereignty laws where you live? What type of information will they be holding? What about sensor data and monitoring data? How will the data be backed up? What communications are necessary to support storage and backup? What is data-deduplication, and why is it important?*

Documentation and Presentation: Students should document their server and networking equipment sizing process, including the analysis of capacity planning, server configurations, networking equipment selections, and cost optimization considerations. They should present their findings and recommendations to the class, explaining their sizing decisions and how they aligned with the data center requirements.

Show students examples of network diagrams and have them create diagrams for their network connectivity inside and outside of the data center. Give examples of the types of information that they are storing. How are the various class projects alike and different?

This project provides students with practical experience in sizing servers and networking equipment for data centers. It allows them to apply their knowledge of capacity planning, performance requirements, and cost optimization to real-world scenarios. Through research, analysis, and documentation, students gain a deeper understanding of the factors involved in effectively sizing equipment in data center environments.

CLOUD

Project: Exploring the Cloud: Understanding Cloud Computing Concepts and Services

Objective: This project aims to help students understand the fundamentals of cloud computing, explore various cloud services, and gain practical experience in utilizing cloud resources.

Steps for the Project:

Research: Instruct students to research the basics of cloud computing, including its definition, characteristics, benefits, and deployment models (public, private, hybrid, and community clouds). Students should familiarize themselves with key concepts like virtualization, elasticity, scalability, and service models (IaaS, PaaS, SaaS).

Cloud Service Comparison: Divide students into groups and assign each group a specific cloud service model (IaaS, PaaS, or SaaS). Instruct them to research and compare popular cloud service providers (Amazon Web Services, Microsoft Azure, or Google Cloud Platform) that offer the assigned service model. Students should evaluate features, pricing, support, scalability, and case studies of real-world applications.

Cloud Use Case Analysis: Provide students with several real-world scenarios that can benefit from cloud computing. These scenarios can include small businesses, educational institutions, or nonprofit organizations. In groups, students should analyze each use case, identify the specific cloud service model(s) that would best suit the scenario, and explain the advantages and challenges associated with using the cloud in that context. Create a class "application." What is the application and what type of data will be stored? What are the security considerations for each type of data? What other aaS type services would be helpful i.e., disaster recovery, business continuity, database?

Cloud Resource Utilization: Introduce students to a cloud service provider's platform (e.g., AWS, Azure, or GCP) and guide them through hands-on exercises. Students should create accounts, provision virtual machines (IaaS), deploy applications (PaaS), or explore pre-built software solutions (SaaS). They should gain practical experience using the cloud platform, understanding resource allocation, and managing cloud resources. If this is too advanced for your students, you can walk through the various selection criteria for cloud resources. What are they and what do they mean?

Cloud Security and Compliance: Instruct students to research and analyze the security considerations associated with cloud computing. They should explore topics such as data protection, encryption, identity and access management, and regulatory compliance. In addition, students should identify best practices for securing cloud-based applications and data and explain how organizations can address security concerns when migrating to the cloud.

Cost Optimization and Governance: Challenge students to explore strategies for optimizing cloud costs and implementing governance in a cloud environment. They should learn about tools and techniques for monitoring resource usage, implementing cost controls, and establishing resource allocation and access management policies. Students should propose cost optimization and governance measures for a given cloud use case. What steps are needed for data sovereignty? How do they vary from country to country. or state to state?

Documentation and Presentation: Students should document their research findings, use case analyses, hands-on experiences, and recommendations. They should create a presentation to share their understanding of cloud computing concepts, compare cloud service models, showcase their hands-on exercises, and discuss their insights on security, cost optimization, and governance.

By researching, analyzing real-world scenarios, and gaining hands-on experience with cloud platforms and terminology, students develop a comprehensive understanding of the cloud's capabilities, benefits, and challenges.

Cloud may be too advanced for some classes, however it is important for students to understand that clouds operate in data centers.

QUALITY ASSURANCE AND ROOT CAUSE. ANALYSIS

Quality assurance is important throughout their career and regardless of industry. Root Cause Analysis is a methodical approach to determining the underlying causes of a problem. As a result, students gain knowledge of problem-solving mechanisms usable throughout their careers.

Objective: This project aims to introduce students to root cause analysis and develop their problem-solving and critical thinking skills by applying root cause analysis techniques to real-world classroom scenarios.

Steps for the Project:

Introduction to Root Cause Analysis: Begin by providing students with an overview of root cause analysis and its importance in problem-solving. Explain the purpose of identifying underlying causes rather than focusing on symptoms. Then, introduce common root cause analysis methodologies such as the "5 Whys" technique or fishbone diagrams (Ishikawa diagrams). Who would they interview? For the classroom problem, should all students be involved? If there was a supervisor in the class, how would they supervise the exercise?

Real-World Classroom Scenarios: Present students with real-world classroom scenarios involving recurring issues or problems. These scenarios can include challenges related to student performance, classroom management, communication, or any other relevant aspects of the learning environment. Choose open-ended scenarios that require deeper analysis to identify the root causes. Alternatively, pick a local problem and have students analyze a solution.

Group Work: Divide students into small groups and assign each group a different classroom scenario to analyze. Instruct them to apply root cause analysis techniques to identify the underlying causes of the problem. Encourage students to ask probing questions, examine various factors, and consider multiple perspectives.

Data Collection and Analysis: Instruct each group to collect data related to the assigned scenario. This may involve conducting interviews, surveys, observations, or analyzing existing data. Students should investigate the data to identify patterns, trends, and potential factors contributing to the problem.

Root Cause Steps: Using the data and analysis, students should apply root cause analysis techniques to determine the root causes of the identified problem. They should utilize tools like the "5 Whys" or fishbone diagrams to dig deeper and uncover the underlying factors contributing to the problem.

1. Determine the problem.
2. Gather information from all stakeholders.
3. Determine the root cause.
4. Find corrective or preventative actions.
5. Draft the corrective actions and train personnel.
6. Monitor and measure to ensure the solution has the intended benefits.
7. Lather, rinse and repeat as needed.
8. Document the final outcomes and publish them to the team.

Solution Development: Once the root causes are identified, instruct students to brainstorm potential solutions or interventions to address the problem. Encourage them to think creatively and consider both short-term and long-term solutions. Students should address the root causes rather than solely managing the symptoms.

Presentation and Discussion: Have each group present their findings, including the identified root causes and proposed solutions. Encourage class discussion and peer feedback to foster critical thinking and further explore alternative perspectives and potential additional root causes.

PROJECT MANAGEMENT

Project Management is used throughout the industry, from construction to the cloud. Methodical steps and documentation ensure the success of projects. The key is the management and, more importantly, the communication between all involved. Students will gain an understanding of the terminology and methodology involved in a project. Below are sample projects for both waterfall and SCRUM methodologies.

Introduce students to the two variations of project management. The main differences are as follows.

- **Project Structure:**
  - *Waterfall: Waterfall follows a sequential, linear approach where each phase (requirements, design, development, testing, deployment) completes one after the other. It has a fixed scope and timeline. Show students and example of a waterfall project. Milestone Gantt chart.*
  - *Scrum: Scrum follows an iterative and incremental approach. The project is divided into smaller time-boxed iterations called sprints, typically lasting 1-4 weeks. Each sprint involves the complete cycle of planning, development, testing, and review. The idea is to catch and fix problems early.*
- **Flexibility and Adaptability:**
  - *Waterfall: Waterfall is rigid and does not adapt well once a phase completes. Any changes requested after the initial planning stage*

may require revisiting previous steps. Having to move back within the project can be costly and time-consuming.

○ *Scrum: Scrum embraces change and is flexible and adaptable by design. It allows adjustments and modifications during each sprint based on feedback and changing requirements.*

- **Communication and Collaboration:**

○ *Waterfall: Waterfall typically involves limited collaboration between team members, clearly separating roles and responsibilities. Communication is primarily top-down, and team members may have limited interaction until their phase begins.*

○ *Scrum: Scrum emphasizes collaboration and cross-functional teamwork. It encourages daily stand-up meetings where team members communicate progress, discuss challenges, and coordinate their work. In addition, close collaboration promotes transparency and knowledge sharing.*

- **Requirements and Documentation:**

○ *Waterfall: Waterfall relies heavily on upfront planning and documentation. Extensive requirements gathering, system design, and documentation are done in the initial phases to provide a comprehensive development plan.*

○ *Scrum: Scrum focuses on delivering working software incrementally. While requirements are still defined, they are not as detailed upfront. Documentation is minimal, with more emphasis on in-person communications.*

- **Customer Engagement:**

○ *Waterfall: Waterfall typically involves limited customer involvement until the final product is delivered. Feedback and customer validation occur at the end of the development cycle or project.*

○ *Scrum: Scrum promotes frequent customer involvement and feedback throughout the development process. Regular reviews and demonstrations of working software are conducted at the end of each sprint, allowing for early customer feedback and validation.*

2. **Risk Management:**

   ○ *Waterfall: Waterfall aims to identify and mitigate risks early in the project through extensive planning. However, changes or unforeseen risks during later phases can be challenging to address.*

   ○ *Scrum: Scrum addresses risks iteratively by identifying and addressing them within each sprint. The short iterations allow for quick adaptation and risk mitigation as the project progresses.*

Both methodologies have their strengths and are suited to different project scenarios. The waterfall is better suited for projects with well-defined and stable requirements. At the same time, Scrum is well-suited for projects with evolving or uncertain requirements requiring flexibility and frequent collaboration.

SCRUM Example Project

SCRUM Objective: This project aims to introduce students to the Scrum methodology and provide hands-on experience using Scrum principles to manage and execute a classroom project.

Steps for the Project:

- **Introduction to Scrum Methodology:** Begin by providing an overview of Scrum methodology, explaining its agile principles and application in project management. Introduce key Scrum concepts such as Scrum roles (Product Owner, Scrum Master, and Development Team), Scrum artifacts (Product Backlog, Sprint Backlog, and Burndown Chart), and Scrum ceremonies (Sprint Planning, Daily Stand-up, Sprint Review, and Sprint Retrospective).

- **Project Definition:** Define a classroom project that can be completed within a specified timeframe (e.g., creating a presentation, organizing a charity event, or developing a software prototype). Clearly outline the project's objectives, deliverables, and success criteria. Emphasize the importance of a clear and well-defined product vision.
- **Scrum Team Formation:** Form project teams consisting of students who will play the Scrum roles—Product Owner, Scrum Master, and Development Team members. Ensure that each team has a diverse set of skills and expertise.
- **Product Backlog Creation:** Instruct the Product Owners to create a Product Backlog, which is a prioritized list of features, tasks, or user stories that need to be completed to achieve the project objectives. The Product Backlog should be dynamic and evolve as the project progresses.
- **Sprint Planning:** Facilitate a Sprint Planning session where the Product Owners work with their respective Development Teams to select a set of Product Backlog items to be completed during the first sprint. Encourage the teams to estimate the effort required for each task and define their definition of "done" for each item.
- **Sprint Execution:** Allocate a fixed time duration (e.g., 1-2 weeks) for the sprint. Instruct the Development Teams to self-organize and collaborate to complete the selected Product Backlog items. Facilitate Daily Stand-up meetings where team members share progress, discuss obstacles, and plan their work for the day.
- **Sprint Review:** At the end of the sprint, conduct a Sprint Review session where each team presents their completed deliverables to the class and stakeholders (if applicable). Encourage feedback and discussion.

- **Sprint Retrospective:** Facilitate a Sprint Retrospective session where each team reflects on their performance during the sprint. Discuss what went well, what challenges were faced, and areas for improvement. Encourage the teams to identify action items for process enhancement in subsequent sprints.
- **Iterative Sprint Execution:** Repeat Steps 5-8 for multiple sprints until the project objectives are met, or the designated timeframe is completed. Emphasize the iterative nature of Scrum and the continuous improvement mindset.
- **Project Closure:** Conduct a final project review session where each team presents their overall project outcomes, lessons learned, and future recommendations. Reflect on the effectiveness of Scrum methodology in managing the classroom project.

Students will gain practical experience in applying Scrum methodology to project management by engaging in this project. In addition, they will develop teamwork, collaboration, time management, communication, and adaptability skills. The project also fosters critical thinking, problem-solving, and reflection through the various Scrum ceremonies and continuous improvement practices.

Waterfall Example Project

Waterfall Objective: This project aims to introduce students to the Waterfall methodology and provide hands-on experience using sequential project management techniques to plan and execute a classroom project.

Steps for the Project:

- **Introduction to Waterfall Methodology:** Begin by providing an overview of the Waterfall methodology and its sequential approach to project management. Explain the distinct phases of the Waterfall model, including requirements gathering, design, implementation, testing, deployment, and maintenance.

- **Project Definition:** Define a classroom project that can be completed within a specified timeframe (e.g., creating a research paper, designing a marketing campaign, or organizing a school event). Clearly outline the project's objectives, deliverables, and success criteria.
- **Requirements Gathering:** Instruct students to conduct thorough research and gather detailed requirements for the project. Students should identify stakeholders, define project scope, and document specific functional and non-functional requirements.
- **Design Phase:** Guide students in creating a comprehensive project plan and design. Instruct them to break down the project into smaller tasks, determine task dependencies, and develop a project schedule or Gantt chart. Emphasize the importance of detailed planning and sequencing of project activities.
- **Implementation Phase:** Divide the students into project teams based on their areas of expertise or interest. Assign each group specific tasks to be completed within the project. Then, instruct the teams to execute their assigned duties according to the project plan and design.
- **Testing Phase:** Instruct the teams to thoroughly test their deliverables against the defined requirements. Emphasize the importance of quality assurance and validation processes. Encourage students to document and address any identified defects or issues.
- **Deployment Phase:** Instruct the teams to prepare their final deliverables for deployment or presentation. Ensure all project requirements have been met and the deliverables are ready for use or evaluation.

- **Project Review and Evaluation:** Conduct a review session where each team presents their completed deliverables and overviews their project journey. Evaluate the project outcomes against the defined success criteria and project requirements.
- **Lessons Learned:** Facilitate a discussion on the strengths and limitations of the Waterfall methodology based on the student's experiences. Encourage students to reflect on the challenges faced during the project and identify potential improvements or alternative approaches for future projects.
- **Project Closure:** Conclude the project with a final reflection session where students discuss their overall project experiences, lessons learned, and recommendations for applying the Waterfall methodology in different contexts.

By engaging in this project, students will gain practical experience using the Waterfall methodology for project management. In addition, they will develop skills in requirements gathering, project planning, task execution, quality assurance, and project evaluation. The project also encourages critical thinking, problem-solving, and reflection on the sequential nature of the Waterfall methodology and its applicability in different project scenarios.

Overall

How are the two project scenarios different? When do you think one would be used more than another? How do students rate their participation preferences?

CODING AND DATABASE MANAGEMENT

Both of these topics are generally covered in other classes and, as such, are not heavily covered in the book. However, understanding how data centers work and power requirements can help coders write better code and programs. If you are using this text with a coding or database class, this is an excellent time to work with students to understand the data center side of coding. This is where their code "lives."

Have students discuss their code and the best means for distribution. Would they prefer to control the assets? Would the prefer to use the cloud? Why for either scenario. What additional measures are they considering due to their placement preferences? Would they write differently for cloud native? How would they change their methodology if an application was going to start in the cloud and move to an in-house facility?

EXERCISE IN SUSTAINABILITY

A good exercise for students to learn about sustainability in data centers could be a sustainability audit. The activity below is listed for a data center, but a student's home could also provide the data points for this project. Here's how you can structure the activity:

- **Introduction to Sustainability in Data Centers:**
    - Begin by providing an overview of the importance of sustainability in data centers, including topics such as energy consumption, carbon emissions, electronic waste, circular economy, and resource management.
    - Explain the potential environmental impact of data centers and the need for sustainable practices to minimize their ecological footprint.
- **Research and Analysis:**
    - Divide students into groups and assign each group a specific focus on sustainability in data centers.
        1. *Energy efficiency, renewable energy adoption, waste management, water conservation, or carbon usage.*
    - Instruct students to research and gather information about best practices, industry standards, case studies, or vendor whitepapers. Students may wish to network with others in the industry for help.

- Students should analyze the current state of sustainability in data centers, identifying challenges and opportunities for improvement. Specifically, what about older equipment? How could students improve power, cooling, and compute to make them move efficient?
- **Sustainability Audit:**
  - Using the information gathered, have each group conduct a sustainability audit of a hypothetical or existing data center. They should evaluate the data center's performance in their assigned aspect of sustainability.
  - Provide students with criteria or metrics to assess the data center's sustainability practices. Metrics could include energy usage, cooling efficiency, recycling programs, adoption of renewable energy sources, etc.
  - Students should document their findings, noting areas where the data center excels and areas that require improvement.
- **Recommendations and Action Plan:**
  - Based on their audit results, each group should develop recommendations and an action plan for the data center to enhance its sustainability practices.
  - Encourage students to think creatively and propose feasible solutions, such as optimizing server utilization, implementing virtualization, adopting energy-efficient cooling systems, or exploring renewable energy sources.
  - Students should present their recommendations and action plans, highlighting the potential environmental impact, and costs versus cost savings associated with their proposals.
- **Discussion and Reflection:**
  - Facilitate a class discussion where students can share their findings, recommendations, and insights from the exercise.

- The importance of sustainability in data centers and how sustainable practices can contribute to a more environmentally responsible and efficient operation should be addressed.
- Discuss the challenges and opportunities of implementing sustainability measures in data centers and explore potential strategies for overcoming those challenges.

By engaging in this exercise, students will learn about sustainability in data centers and develop critical thinking, research, and problem-solving skills while considering the environmental impact of technology infrastructure.

ALTERNATE EXERCISES IN SUSTAINABILITY AND CARBON ACCOUNTABILITY

Have students use their digital diaries (or create one). List all communications and internet transactions for a period of time. The larger the sampling, the better. Have students tally up the various types of communications as follows:

- Application
- Total number of minutes
- Estimated power for one (web search or estimate)
- Total power for the day
- Total power for the year
- Total number of users of that application
- Estimated total power for all. (Alternatively, students may use estimates or home power bills).
- Total annual power for the average home in your country
- How many homes could be powered with the same power above?
- What about an average hospital? School?
- Other ways to use power in calculations? What if their home moved to another area o the country? What would their carbon source makeup be at that point? How many trees would they need to plant to offset their technology (or household) footprint?

Estimating the power consumption for a single person's use of Twitter over a year involves several variables and assumptions. For example, here's a rough estimate based on the average power usage of devices:

- Device Power Consumption:
  - Let's assume a smartphone or computer consumes an average of 5-10 watts of power while actively using Twitter.
- Daily Usage:
  - Assuming an average usage of 30 minutes per day on Twitter.
- Annual Usage:
  - Multiply the daily usage by 365 days to get the annual usage.

Now, let's calculate the power consumption for a single person using Twitter for a year based on these assumptions:

- *Minimum Power Consumption: 5 watts * 0.5 hours = 2.5 watt-hours per day*
- *Maximum Power Consumption: 10 watts * 0.5 hours = 5 watt-hours per day*
- *Annual Power Consumption: 2.5 watt-hours * 365 days = 912.5 watt-hours (or 0.9125 kilowatt-hours) 5 watt-hours * 365 days = 1,825 watt-hours (or 1.825 kilowatt-hours)*

Other estimates that can be used.

- Annual Power Consumption of a User on the Internet in the USA (try a few countries).
- (Total amount of power used by all data centers in your country / devices) x number of devices in use.

- Power for one SNAP (or other apps) x number of users in an internet minute x minutes in a year. Convert to kW/h / average power usage for a home = number of homes

It's important to note that these are rough estimates and can vary significantly based on individual usage patterns, the type of devices used, and their power efficiency. Moreover, power consumption can vary when considering activities such as multimedia content consumption, browsing external links, or using additional applications simultaneously with Twitter. This estimate only considers the power the device consumes while actively using Twitter. It does not consider the energy consumed by the network infrastructure, data centers, or other components involved in delivering the service. Web searches and assumptions can help students glean data center power consumption.

What other ways can you suggest students evaluate their carbon footprint for computing?

HARDWARE POWER CALCULATIONS

Have students select various hardware products and calculate power consumption based on various factors such as packets passed, speed, users supported, number of users per core, and power per port. Then, try to figure out the power consumption for an entire internet conversation.

- How did students arrive at their calculations?
- How could they improve power? For example, would a greater number of lower-power servers be better than one large server?
- What are the pros and cons of more versus fewer servers?
    - *Number of power connections, number of cabling connections, fewer network ports, more competition for resources, number of users that could go down at one time, cost for software, and resiliency.*
- Have students research how to evaluate power consumption for data center components. Assign various specialties to students. Have them determine how to assess power on one model versus another.

EXTRAS AND RESOURCES

This section of the book lists organizations, standards, scholarships, and other helpful information. The book also showcases organizations that have student chapters and ones that will be useful as they work through their careers. There are also about 300 different job titles and descriptions. Students can look up the various organizations and job descriptions to better understand the industry. The website https://www.internationaldatacenterday.com has many interviews with people in the industry and the podcast *"Jumpstart Your Career in Data Centers."* There are also scholarship resources in the book. https://www.carriegoetz.com will be updated with new resources as they become available. You can also request a meeting to discuss ideas and provide feedback, or request a talk with your class. If you need data center professionals to speak to your class, many organizations would be happy to help. Most are listed in the book's resources section.

www.ingramcontent.com/pod-product-compliance
Lightning Source LLC
Chambersburg PA
CBHW040929210326
41597CB00030B/5240